WE COME FROM

Jamaica

ALISON BROWNLIE

HODDER
Wayland

an imprint of Hodder Children's Books

WE COME FROM

Brazil • China • France
Germany • India • Jamaica • Japan
Kenya • Nigeria • South Africa

The people you are about to meet live in a town in Jamaica called Spanish Town. Like any country, Jamaica has many different types of lifestyle. People live in the countryside as well as in towns and cities.

Cover: Jo-Ann and Kyle with one of their friends.

Title page top to bottom: The beach at Montego Bay; a tourist guide with a tropical flower; a street in Kingston; a worker on a banana plantation; a bauxite mine near Mandeville.

Contents page: Boys practise their football skills.

Index: Jo-Ann waves goodbye.

**All Wayland books encourage
children to read and help them improve their literacy.**

✓ The contents page, page numbers, headings and index help locate specific pieces of information.

✓ The glossary reinforces alphabetic knowledge and extends vocabulary.

✓ The further information section suggests other books dealing with the same subject.

Series editor: Katie Orchard
Book editor: Alison Cooper
Designer: Jean Wheeler
Production controller: Tracy Fewtrell

Picture Acknowledgements: Alison Brownlie 10 (bottom), 20 (bottom); Eye Ubiquitous/David Cumming 14 (bottom); John Wright 17 (top). All the other photographs in this book were taken by Howard Davies. The map artwork on the title page and page 5 is by Peter Bull.

First published in 1999 by
Wayland Publishers Limited
61 Western Road, Hove
East Sussex, BN3 1JD, England

This paperback edition published in 2002
by Hodder Wayland

© Copyright 1999 Wayland Publishers Limited

British Library Cataloguing in Publication Data
Brownlie, Alison 1949–
  We come from Jamaica
  1. Jamaica – Geography – Juvenile literature
  2. Jamaica – Social conditions – Juvenile literature
  I. Title II. Jamaica
  972.9'2'06

ISBN 0 7502 4388 0

Typeset by Jean Wheeler, England
Printed and bound in Hong Kong

Contents

Welcome to Jamaica!

'My name is Jo-Ann. Here I am with my mother and father and my little brother, Kyle, who is 6.'

Jo-Ann Johnson is 8 years old. She lives with her family in Leiba Gardens, a suburb of Spanish Town. Spanish Town is the third-largest town in Jamaica, after Kingston and Montego Bay. You can see where all these towns are on the map on page 5.

▲ *From left to right: Mr Johnson, Kyle, Jo-Ann and Mrs Johnson.*

▶ *Jamaica's place in the world.*

▼ *Jamaica is an island in the Caribbean Sea.*

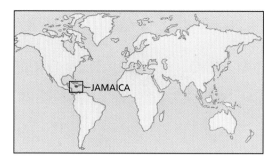

▲ *Jamaica's place in the world.*

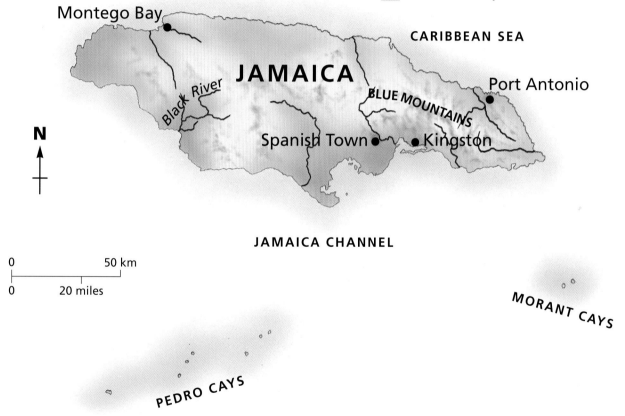

JAMAICA	
Capital city	Kingston
Land area	11,000 square kilometres
Population	2.5 million people
Main language	English
Main religion	Christianity

The Land and Weather

Most of Jamaica is hilly, and in some places the land is too steep to grow crops. Around Spanish Town, where Jo-Ann lives, it is much flatter. Farmers grow sugar-cane in the countryside around the town.

▶ *Tourists take boat trips along the Black River.*

▼ *This ferry carries passengers across Kingston Harbour. It is one of the biggest harbours in the world.*

▶ *Some parts of the island are covered with thick, green forests.*

7

These are coffee beans. The weather in Jamaica is good for growing coffee.

It is hot in Jamaica all year round. Sometimes there is heavy rain, which can cause flooding. It rains more often in the north of the island than it does in the south. The rain helps plants to grow, so the northern part of Jamaica looks very green.

Parts of this house sank into the ground after an earthquake in 1907.

‘We have a lot of sunshine in Jamaica but we also have big storms, and sometimes even hurricanes.’ Kyle.

9

At Home

Most people in Jamaica live in houses rather than flats. In the countryside, houses are usually quite small. They have wooden walls, and the roofs are made from corrugated metal. As the weather is warm all year round, people spend most of their time outside.

▼ *People sometimes build their own houses. This one is near Port Antonio.*

▲ *Jo-Ann and Kyle spend a lot of time playing in their garden.*

▶ *These luxury houses are in Red Hills, a suburb of Kingston.*

10

11

▶ *Kingston is a busy city with tall office blocks and hotels.*

Many people have moved to the towns to find jobs. The poorest people live in shanty towns on the edges of Kingston and Spanish Town. Wealthier people, like Jo-Ann's family, live in suburbs.

▼ *Jo-Ann's family can afford to have a television and a microwave oven.*

'In our new house I will have my own bedroom where I can keep all my books.' Jo-Ann.

Jo-Ann's house is quite small and she has to share a room with her brother, Kyle. Soon the family is going to move to a new house, and everyone will have more space.

Jamaican Food

Jamaicans like food that is spicy and peppery. Jerk chicken is a tasty chicken dish, cooked over a wood fire. The national dish is salt fish and ackee. Many different kinds of fish are caught in the sea around the island.

▼ *Jerk chicken is often cooked and sold by the roadside.*

▲ *Ackee is a fruit. It can give off a poisonous gas when it is opened.*

14

'I like sandwiches, but my favourite meal is rice, peas and chicken.' Jo-Ann.

Long hours of sunshine and heavy rain help crops to grow well in Jamaica. People who live in the countryside often grow their own fruit and vegetables.

▲ *Bananas are kept in plastic bags while they are growing, to keep insects out.*

'I chop open the coconuts so people can taste the coconut milk – it's delicious and very good for you!' Market trader.

▲ *At the market, people sell the fruit and vegetables they have grown.*

In the towns, people buy food from market stalls, as well as from modern shopping malls. Yams, breadfruit, coconuts, plantain and mangoes are favourite foods.

At Work

In the countryside, many people work on plantations. They grow foods such as pineapples and bananas, which are sold to other countries.

Many Jamaicans work in hotels, looking after people who come to the island for their holidays. Jo-Ann's mother works for the Jamaica Tourist Board in Kingston.

▲ *This Rastafarian man sells souvenirs to holidaymakers.*

▼ *Bananas are washed and packed into boxes. Then they are loaded on to ships.*

'I like meeting people from different countries. I am very proud of Jamaica.' Beverley Johnson, Jo-Ann's mother.

At School

All children up to the age of 11 go to school. Then, if they pass an exam, they can go on to secondary school. Some children do not go to secondary school because their parents cannot afford it.

▲ *All schoolchildren have to wear a school uniform.*

▶ *These children have some of their work displayed on the classroom wall.*

◀ *A school for Rastafarian children.*

▲ *Jo-Ann's teacher helps her with some work on the board.*

School starts early in the morning, when it is still cool. It finishes at around half-past one in the afternoon. Jamaican children have to do a lot of homework after school.

◄ *A girl gets ready to throw the ball in a school netball match.*

Jo-Ann's favourite subjects are English, Maths and Religious Education. She is learning Spanish too, which she thinks is fun, but hard work. Sometimes she works on the computer – nearly all schools in Jamaica have them.

'I enjoy reading stories about Robin Hood. Sometimes I read them out loud for Kyle.' Jo-Ann.

Free Time

Sports such as football, baseball and basketball are very popular. In towns and cities, people often join sports clubs and youth clubs. Children in the countryside play games anywhere they can.

At weekends families like to spend time together. Both adults and children enjoy watching television.

▲ *Some families go to church together on Sundays.*

▶ *These boys are enjoying a game of basketball.*

'I go to Brownies every Thursday. All my friends go too. We have a great time!' Jo-Ann.

Looking Ahead

Jamaica is a beautiful and lively country. People enjoy coming here for their holidays, and this provides jobs for Jamaican people. But some people worry that the island will be spoilt if too many hotels are built.

▼ *Jamaica's beaches may be spoiled if too many people come here.*

▲ *Luxury yachts in Kingston harbour.*

'When I am older, I would like to work in the tourist industry, like my mum.' Jo-Ann.

Sky Juice Recipe

Sky juice is made from fruits that grow all over Jamaica.

Ingredients

6 Oranges

1 Grapefruit

1 Tin pineapple pieces

Ice cubes

Equipment

2 Tall glasses

Knife

Lemon squeezer

Jug

Rolling pin

▲ *Jo-Ann squeezes an orange.*

1. Slice the grapefruit and oranges in half and squeeze the juice into the jug using the squeezer.

2. Wrap the ice cubes in a tea towel and crush them with the rolling pin.

3. Put the crushed ice in the glasses.

4. Pour in the juice, add the pineapple pieces and enjoy a cool drink with your friends.

▶ *Jo-Ann and Kyle enjoy a refreshing drink of sky juice.*

Jamaica Fact File

◀ Money Facts

Jamaican money is the Jamaican dollar. There are 100 cents in one dollar. Four Jamaican dollars are about the same as £1.

The Jamaican Motto

The motto is 'Out of many, one people'. Jamaican people's ancestors came from many different places, including Africa, Europe and Southeast Asia. Now they are all Jamaicans.

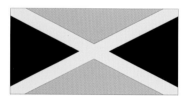

The Jamaican Flag

◀ Each of the colours on the Jamaican flag has a special meaning – green for the land, yellow for the sun and black for the people.

Famous Jamaicans

The reggae ▶ musician Bob Marley was a very famous Jamaican. He died in 1981. Marcus Garvey was a Jamaican who worked hard to make Jamaica free and independent.

Sport

Merlene Ottey is a Jamaican runner who has won Olympic gold medals. The Jamaican football team became famous in 1998 when it reached the final rounds of the World Cup for the first time.

Highest Peak

Jamaica's highest ▶ mountain is called the Blue Mountain Peak and it is 2,256 metres high.

Place Names

Many places in Jamaica have the same names as places in the UK. Look at a map and see how many you can find.

Longest River

▲ Jamaica's longest river is the Black River, which is 22.5 kilometres long. It is home to the Jamaican crocodile.

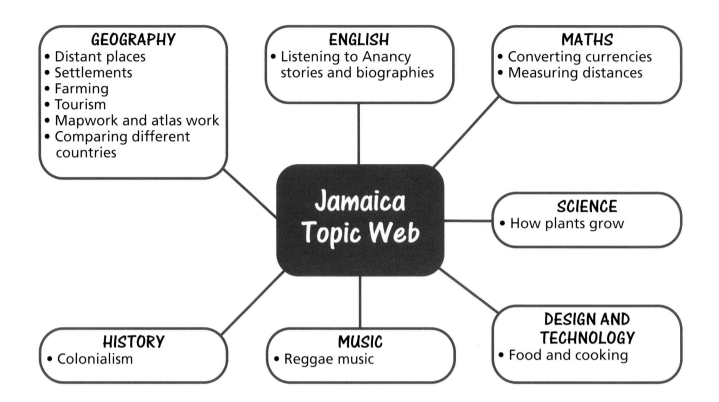

GEOGRAPHY
- Distant places
- Settlements
- Farming
- Tourism
- Mapwork and atlas work
- Comparing different countries

ENGLISH
- Listening to Anancy stories and biographies

MATHS
- Converting currencies
- Measuring distances

Jamaica Topic Web

SCIENCE
- How plants grow

DESIGN AND TECHNOLOGY
- Food and cooking

HISTORY
- Colonialism

MUSIC
- Reggae music

Extension Activities

GEOGRAPHY
- Find Jamaica in an atlas.
- Ask the children to make a list of all the similarities between their own lives and Jo-Ann's.

ENGLISH
- Ask the children to imagine they are on holiday in Jamaica. What would they write on a postcard home? What is Jamaica like?

LITERACY HOUR
- Use this book as an example of non-fiction, a book about Bob Marley as biography and a story (perhaps an Anancy story) as an example of fiction from another culture.

ART
- Design a poster advertising Jamaica as a holiday island.

MUSIC
- Listen to reggae music and clap out the rhythm.

INFORMATION TECHNOLOGY
- Find out more information about Jamaica from the Internet.

HISTORY
- Find out which countries the people of Jamaica came from.

Glossary

Corrugated metal Thin, wavy sheets of metal.

Harbours Places where ships and boats can be loaded and unloaded.

Plantations Large farms where crops are grown to be sold to other countries.

Rastafarian Someone who believes Haile Selassie, who was emperor of Ethiopia, is a god.

Reggae music A type of music that developed in the Caribbean. It is now popular in many countries.

Shanty towns Areas of very poor houses on the edge of a large town or city.

Souvenirs Things that people buy to remind them of a place they have visited.

Suburb An area of houses on the edge of a town or city.

Further Information

Fiction:

Anancy Spiderman: Twenty Caribbean Folk Stories by James Berry (Walker, 1989)

Caribbean Stories by Robert Hull (Wayland, 1994)

Multicultural Stories: Caribbean by Paul Dash (Wayland, 1999)

Non-fiction:

Country Insights: Jamaica by Alison Brownlie (Wayland, 1997)

A Flavour of the Caribbean by Linda Illsley (Wayland, 1998)

Worldfocus Jamaica by John Barraclough (Heinemann/Oxfam, 1995)

Organizations:

Jamaica Tourist Board, 1-2 Prince Consort Road, London SW7 2BZ

Index

All the numbers in **bold** refer to illustrations.